ALCOHOL AND TOBACCO TAX AND TRADE BUREAU

2007
FEDERAL COMPLIANCE TRAINING
FOR THE
BREWERY INDUSTRY

TTB P 5130.005 (09/2007)

TTB Brewery Compliance Seminar

Objective: At the end of this seminar, participants will be able to maintain required records and correctly file reports and tax returns.

TTB P 5130.005 (09/2007)

ALCOHOL AND TOBACCO TAX AND TRADE BUREAU
OFFICE CONTACT LIST

Alcohol & Tobacco Tax and Trade Bureau
1301 G. Street, NW, Washington, D.C. 20220   (202)-927-5000

Advertising, Labeling and Formulation Division   (202)-927-8140
                            Toll Free   (866)-927-2533

Regulations & Procedures Division   (202)-927-8210

Beer Industry Analyst   Industyanalyst.beer@ttb.gov   (202)-302-3856

Technical Advisor for Beer   ████████   (513)-684-6130
                              Toll Free   (877)-882-3277

San Francisco Laboratory Center, Walnut Creek, CA   (925)-280-3600
                                      Fax: (925)-280-3601

Pay.gov   Pay.gov@ttb.gov   Toll Free   (877)-882-3277
                                                        Option #6

Correspondence, Operational Reports and Applications from
alcohol and tobacco operations such as Distilled Spirits Plants,
Breweries, Wineries, Wholesalers and Importers should be directed to:
> **National Revenue Center**
> **Federal Office Building, Room 8002**
> **550 Main Street**
> **Cincinnati, OH.　45202-3263**
> **Telephone:　　(513)-684-3334**
> **Toll Free:　　(800)-398-2282**

Excise Tax Returns should be sent to:
> **TTB**
> **Excise Tax**
> **P.O. Box 790353**
> **St. Louis, MO　63179**

Applications for Label Approvals and Formulas should be sent to:
> **Advertising, Labeling and Formulation Division**
> **1310 G. Street NW**
> **Washington, D.C. 20220**

Visit us on the web at: www.ttb.gov

Brewer's Report of Operations

Excise Taxes

TTB P 5130.005 (09/2007)

Records, Reports and Returns

27 CFR 25 Beer

Subpart K - Tax on Beer

Subpart U - Records and Reports

http://ecfr.gpoaccess.gov/

Records

Brewers must have some type of reporting system which captures information about operations throughout the brewery.

Recordkeeping Matters

- Types
- Time of Making Entries
- Record Retention
- Data Processing
- Photographic Copies
- Notice File

TTB P 5130.005 (09/2007)

Sequence

- Daily Records
- Summary Records
- Report of Operations
- Tax Return

Daily Records

- Materials received and used
- Beer produced
- Beer transferred to/from bottling
- Beer transferred to/from racking

Daily Records

- Beer bottled or racked
- Beer removed for consumption or sale
- Beer returned to brewery (offsets)
- Beer destroyed
- Beer lost due to breakage, theft, etc.

Daily Records

- Exports
- Supplies for vessels & aircraft
- Transfer to another brewery
- Research or analysis
- Personal use

Other Records

- Alcohol content
- Fill tests
- Balling
- Record of test of measuring devices

Daily Summary Records

- As the name implies, summaries of the day's activities
- In simplest terms, these records can be a spreadsheet summarizing the information from the source documents

TTB P 5130.005 (09/2007)

Reports of Operations

@ Brewer's Report of Operations, Form 5130.9

@ Brewpub Report of Operations, Form 5130.26

Brewer's Report of Operations

Use if you:

- Produce 5000 bbls or more per year

OR

- Bottle or keg beer

Brewer's Report of Operations

@ File monthly if:

- Produce *more* than *10,000* bbls per year

@ File quarterly if:

- Produce *less* than *10,000* bbls per year

Brewpub Report of Operations

Use if you:

* Produce less than 5,000 bbls per year

   AND

* Do not bottle or keg beer

Excise Tax on Beer

◆ The rate of tax on beer is $18.00 per barrel if the brewer produces more than 2,000,000 barrels of beer per year.

◆ If the brewer produces less than 2,000,000 barrels of beer per year the rate of tax is reduced to $7.00 per barrel on the first 60,000 barrels that are removed for consumption or sale from the brewery.

Excise Tax Return

◆ Semi Monthly   Due Dates
  - 1-15
  - 16-31
    Not later than the 14th day after the last day of the return period

    - See www.ttb.gov

TTB P 5130.005 (09/2007)

Excise Tax Returns

◆ Special Rule for September

  ◆ Third Return Period

   ▪ EFT – See 27 CFR 25. 164
   ▪ Non-FET – See 27 CFR 25. 164

Excise Tax Return

◆ Quarterly Return

   ▪ Criteria - Not more than $50,000 per calendar year in beer tax
   ▪ Bond amount must be 29% of your total tax liability in a calendar year

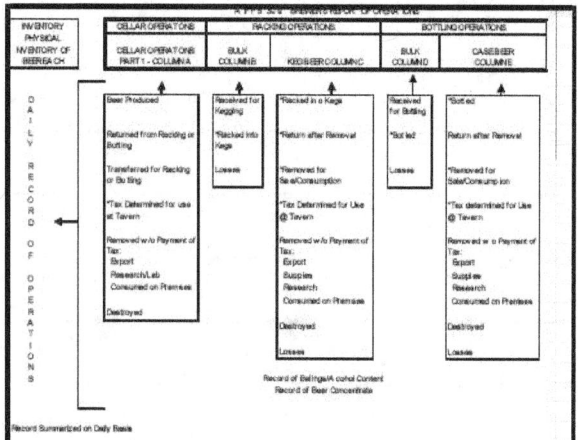

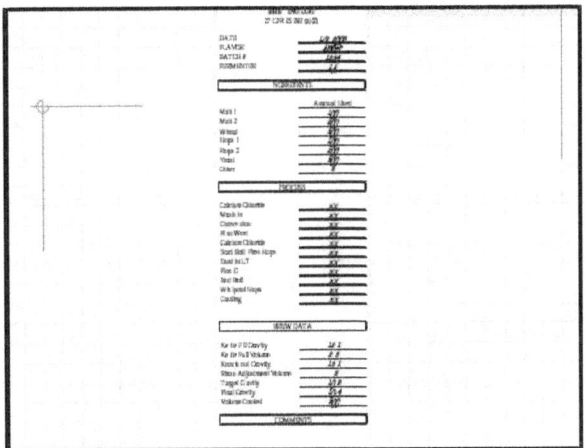

BREW DAY LOG
27 CFR 25.292 (a)(2)

RACKING LOG
27CFR 25.292 (a)(3), (4), (5), (6)

DATE	BARRELS TO RACKING	BARRELS RACKED	LOSSES	AMBER		WHEAT		RASPBERRY		WINTER		IPA	
				1/2	1/4	1/2	1/4	1/2	1/4	1/2	1/4	1/2	1/4
1/3	25.00	25.00	0.00	25.00									
1/4			0.00										
1/5			0.00										
1/6			0.00										
1/7			0.00										
1/10	182.00	180.00	2.00			100.00	80.00						
1/11	75.00	75.00	0.00					75.00					
1/12			0.00										
1/13			0.00										
1/14	5.00	5.00	0.00							5.00			
1/17			0.00										
1/18			0.00										
1/19	55.00	50.00	5.00									50.00	
1/20			0.00										
1/21			0.00										
1/24			0.00										
1/25	100.00	100.00	0.00	75.00	25.00								
1/26			0.00										
1/27			0.00										
1/28	50.00	50.00	0.00										50.00
1/31			0.00										
TOTAL	492.00	485.00	7.00	100.00	25.00	100.00	80.00	75.00	0.00	5.00	0.00	50.00	50.00

BOTTLING LOG
27CFR 25.292 (a)(3), (4), (5), (6)

DATE	BARRELS TO BOTTLING	BARRELS BOTTLED	LOSSES	AMBER		WHEAT		RASPBERRY		WINTER		IPA	
				12/12	12/24	12/12	12/24	12/12	12/24	12/12	12/24	12/12	12/24
1/3	101.00	100.02	0.98	100.02									
1/4			0.00										
1/5	252.00	249.97	2.03			174.99	74.98						
1/8			0.00										
1/9			0.00										
1/10	363.00	341.02	11.98			190.01	55.02	95.99					
1/11	203.00	199.99	3.01					199.99					
1/12			0.00										
1/13			0.00										
1/14	526.00	524.98	1.02							199.99	74.98	199.99	50.01
1/17			0.00										
1/18			0.00										
1/19	498.00	474.97	23.03							399.98	74.98		
1/20			0.00										
1/21			0.00										
1/24			0.00										
1/25	251.00	250.05	0.95	100.02	50.01	100.02							
1/26			0.00										
1/27			0.00										
1/28	102.00	100.02	1.98									100.02	
1/31			0.00										
TOTAL	2296.00	2241.01	44.99	200.04	50.01	405.02	130.00	295.98	0.00	199.99	74.98	700.00	124.99

TTB P 5130.005 (09/2007)

Tax Determined for Use in Tavern
27 CFR 25.25(c)(1) & 25.292(a)(8)

Month: January 2005

DATE	TANK	FLAVOR	BARRELS
1/3/2005	1	Raspberry	50.25
1/4/2005	2	Wheat	62.46
1/6/2005	4	Amber	75.32
1/7/2005	3	IPA	47.30
1/10/2005	1	Winter	55.98
1/11/2005	5	Raspberry	67.85
1/13/2005	2	Wheat	63.98
1/14/2005	3	IPA	45.87
1/17/2005	4	Amber	80.42
1/18/2005	1	Winter	57.94
1/19/2005	3	IPA	35.97
1/21/2005	5	Raspberry	56.47
1/24/2005	2	Wheat	47.94
1/27/2005	3	IPA	58.29
1/31/2005	1	Raspberry	45.98
TOTAL			852.02

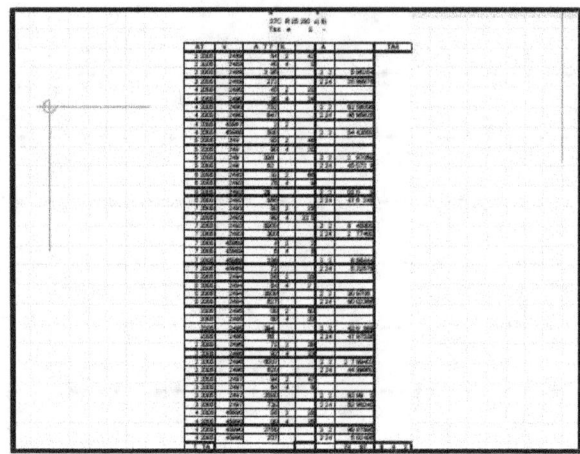

DAILY RETURNED LOG
27 CFR 25.292 (a)(12)

DATE	DESCRIPTION	SIZE	QUANTITY	BARRELS	REASON	REMOVED BY
1/3/2005	Amber	1/2	10	5	bad date	JG
1/10/2005	Raspberry	12/24	96	6.97	bad date	PH
1/12/2005	Wheat	1/4	24	6	bad date	JG
1/19/2005	Winter	12/24	140	10.16	damaged packaging	SH
1/26/2005	Amber	12/24	56	4.06	bad date	PH

DAILY DESTROYED LOG
27 CFR 25.292 (a)(14)

DATE	DESCRIPTION	SIZE	QUANTITY	BARRELS	REASON	REMOVED BY
1/3/2005	Amber	1/2	10	5	bad date	JG
1/5/2005	IPA	1/2	4	2	leaking	SH
1/10/2005	Raspberry	12/24	96	6.97	bad date	PH
1/12/2005	Wheat	1/4	24	6	bad date	JG
1/19/2005	Winter	12/24	140	10.16	damaged packaging	SH
1/26/2005	Amber	12/24	56	4.06	bad date	PH
1/28/2005	Wheat	1/4	4	1	leaking	SH

Inventory

@ Taken at least once each month, within 7 days of end of month

@ Must show:

- Date
- Quantity
- Losses, gains, shortages
- Signature under penalty of perjury by person who took it

TTB P 5130.005 (09/2007)

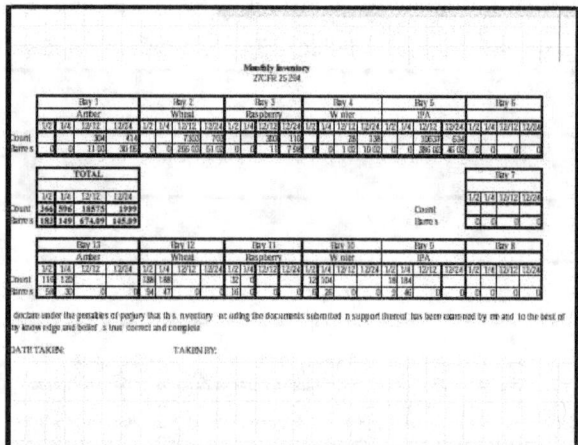

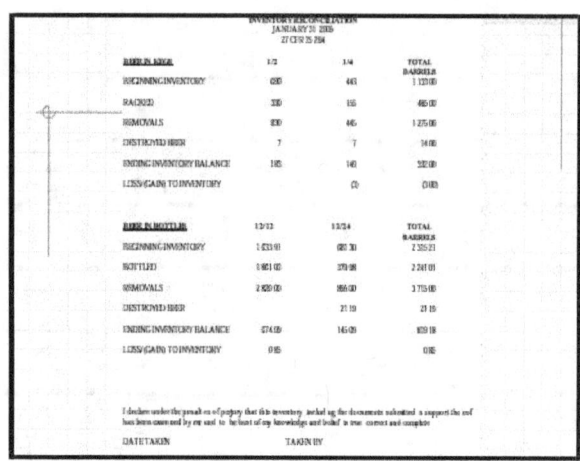

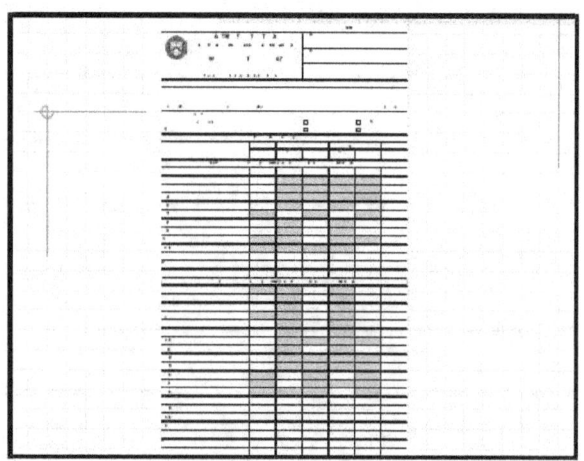

DEPARTMENT OF THE TREASURY

BREWER'S REPORT OF OPERATIONS

12-3456789

-ST-AAA-###

(503) 123-4567

ABC Brewing

123 NE Main St.   Portland   Multnomah   OR   97654

2005

January

Operations	Cans	Racking		Bottling		tota
	(b)					
On hand beginning of this period	3225.00	0.00	1133.00	0.00	2313.21	66 3.21
2 Was caused by fermentation	2000.00					2000.00
3 Weadded water and other liquids in all operations						0.00
4 Beer received from racking and bottling						0.00
5 Beer received outside brewery						0.00
6 Beer received breweries		492.00		2286.00		2778.00
7 Beer returned to this brewery			11.00		21 19	32.19
8 Beer received outside this brewery						0.00
9 Racked			485.00			485.00
0 Bottled					2241.01	2241.01
Physical inventory disclosed an overage			3.00			3.00
1						0.00
2 Total additions to beer inventory	5225.00	492.00	1632.00	2286.00	4577.41	14212.41

Removals from beer inventory (round your entries to the nearest second decimal)

1 Removed for consumption or sale			1275.00		3721.43	4996.43
5 Tax determined for use at taverns on brewery premises	852.02					852.02
16 Removal without payment of tax for export						0.00
17 Removal without payment of tax as supplies (vessels, etc.)						0.00
18 Removal without payment of tax for use in research or						0.00
19 Removed without payment of tax to other breweries and pilot brewing plants						0.00
20 Beer unfit for sale removed for use in manufacturing						0.00
21 Beer consumed on premises						0.00
22 Beer transferred for racking	492.00					492.00
23 Beer transferred for bottling	2286.00					2286.00
2 Beer returned to cellars						0.00
25 Beer racked		485.00				485.00
26 Beer bottled				2241.00		2241.00
27 Laboratory samples						0.00
28 Beer destroyed at brewery			14.00		21 19	35 19
29 Beer transferred to a distilled spirits plant						0.00
30 Recorded losses, including theft		7.00		45.00		52.00
31 Physical inventory disclosed a shortage					0.85	0.85
33						0.00
32 On hand end of period		1594.96	0.00	343.00	0.00	833.94	2771.92
3 Total beer	5225.00	492.00	1632.00	2286.00	4577.41	14212.41

John Smith   Owner   2/12/2005

Serial number	Date	Tax on beer eligible (col × 12)	Adjustments	Amount due
2005-1	1/27 2005	$19,618.48	$45.00	$19,663.48
2005-2	2/12 2005	$21,095.34	-$85.75	$21,009.59

Item	Hops (pounds)	Hops extract (pounds)	Hops equivalent	Wort (barrels)	Malted Barley			
Materials on hand	4076				241,504			
Wort received and used								
Wort removed								

Added		lbs	$		lbs
2 Removed		lbs	$		lbs
3 Recorded wastage		lbs	$		lbs
4 Received options		lbs	On hand end of period		lbs

TTB P 5130.005 (09/2007)

Reconciliation Tax Returns to Report of Operation

Reconciliation Report of Operations to Tax Returns
Jan. 06

Report of Operations

Removed for Consumption or Sale (bbls)		Tax Rate	Total Tax
Kegs	1276		
Cases	3721.45		
Tavern	862.02		
	5840.45	7.00	40899.15
Less Returns as Offsets			
Cases	32.19	7.00	225.33
			40 713.82

Tax Returns

S/N 2006 1		19 616 46
S/N 2006 2		21 095 34
		40 713 82

Note

Adjustments to tax liability are a separate matter

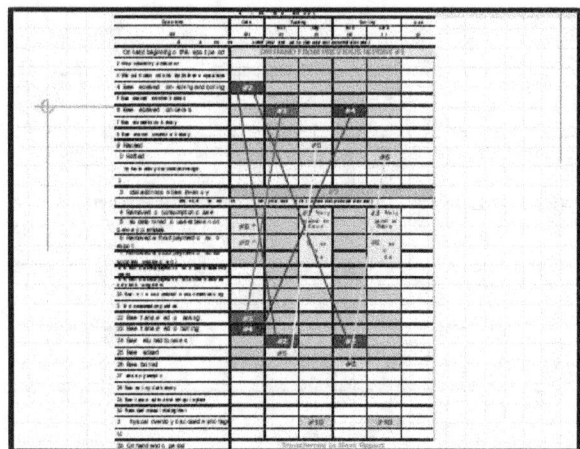

Common Problems

- ☺ You must file a report every period;
- ☺ All entries are in barrels, except Materials Used;
- ☺ Beer for tavern vs. consumed on premises;
- ☺ Don't forget the totals in Column G;
- ☺ Person must have signing authority;
- ☺ Correct headings used in Part 3- refer to Beer Materials Handout

DEPARTMENT OF THE TREASURY
ALCOHOL AND TOBACCO TAX AND TRADE BUREAU (TTB)

OMB No. 1513-0058 (05/31/200_)

BREWPUB REPORT OF OPERATIONS

(You must follow the instructions on the back of this report.)

Our Brewery EIN is:
12-3456789

Our Brewery Number is:
BR ST-AAA-XXX

TTB can reach us by telephone at:
(503) 123-4567

What is your brewery's name?
ABC Brewing

What is the location of your brewery?
123 NE Main St. — Portland — Multnomah — OR — 97654
(Number and Street) — (City) — (County) — (State) — (Zip Code)

Reporting Period (Enter year) 2005
Quarterly Report for

☒ January - March ☐ April - June ☐ July - September ☐ October - December

Part 1 Cellar Operations

Additions to beer inventory	Number of barrels	Removals from beer inventory	Number of barrels
1. Produced by fermentation	470.25	9. Beer tax determined, or use in the tavern	466.25
2. We added water and other liquids in cellar operations		10. Beer transferred to other breweries or pilot brewery	3.75
3. Beer received from other brewers	2.00	12. Beer consumed on premises	
4. Beer returned to our brewery	0.50	13. Beer destroyed at brewery	0.50
5. Physical inventory disclosed an overage		14. Recorded beer losses, including theft (explain in remarks)	2.25
		15. Physical inventory disclosed a shortage (see instruction 5)	
6.		16.	
7. Our total beer to account for (add rows 1 through 7)	472.75	17. Total removals from inventory (add rows 9 through 8)	472.75
8. We adjust from a prior reporting period (explain in Part 5 - Remarks, on back)		18. We adjust from a prior reporting period (explain in Part 5 - Remarks, on back)	2.00

Part 2 Report Period Tax Payments (See Instructions - Part 2)

Return Serial Number	Date Filed	Tax Liability	Adjustments	Amount Paid
2005-1	1/28/2005	$ 105.00	$ -	$ 105.00
2005-2	2/5/2005	$ 890.75	$ 14.00	$ 904.75
2005-3	2/27/2005	$ 546.00	$ -	$ 546.00
2005-4	3/6/2005	$ 348.25	$ -	$ 348.25
2005-5	3/29/2005	$ 698.25	$ -	$ 698.25
2005-6	4/4/2005	$ 675.50	$ -	$ 675.50
		$		$

Part 3 Summary of Materials Used and Wort Produced

Item	Hops (pounds) (a)	Hops Extract (pounds) (b)	Hops Extract Hops Equivalent (c)	Wort (barrels) (d)	Barley specify (e)	Wheat specify (f)	specify (g)	specify (h)
1. Material for beer & cereal beverage	576				25295	3720		
2. Wort received and used								
3. Wort removed								

Under penalties of perjury I declare that this report is supported by true, complete, and correct records that are available for inspection at my brewery. I have examined this report and to the best of my knowledge and belief it is true, complete, and correct.

John Smith — Owner — 4/4/05
(Signature) — (Title) — (Date)

TTB F 5130.20 (200_)

TTB P 5130.005 (09/2007)

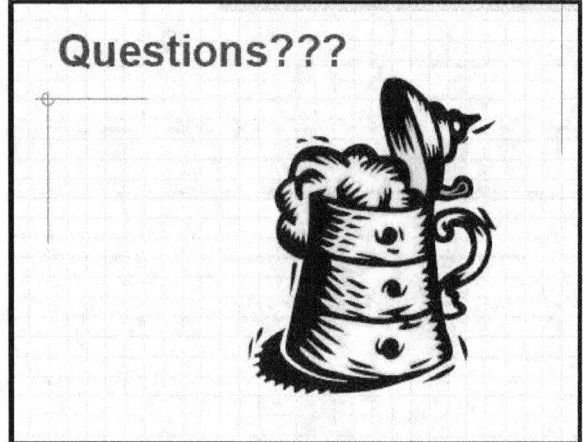

Questions???

_____

_____

_____

_____

_____

_____

_____

RECORDKEEPING
27 CFR 25.291-25.301

Daily Records:

There are a number of records that breweries need to keep on a daily basis. These include:

- Each material received and used in production
- Beer produced
- Beer transferred to and returned from bottling
- Beer transferred to and returned from racking
- Beer bottled
- Beer racked
- Cereal beverage removed
- Beer removed for consumption or sale, including date, person shipped/delivered to and quantity
- Beer removed without payment of tax, include date, person shipped/delivered to and quantity
- Packaged beer used for lab samples
- Beer consumed at brewery
- Beer returned to brewery
- Beer returned to brewery after removal from another brewery owned by same brewer
- Beer reconditioned, used as material or destroyed
- Beer received from other breweries or pilot brewing plants
- Beer lost due to breakage, theft, casualty or other unusual cause
- Brewing materials sold or transferred to pilot brewing plants and used in the manufacture of wort, wort concentrate, malt syrup and malt extract for sale or removal
- Record of tests of measuring devises
- Beer purchased from other brewers in the purchasing brewer's barrels and kegs and such beer sold to other brewers.

Removals Without Payment of Tax:

Another type of record that must be kept is for removals made without payment of tax. Types of removals that fit this category include:

- Exports;
- Supplies for vessels & aircraft;
- Research or analysis;
- Beer returned to brewery;
- Beer destroyed;
- Beer lost due to breakage, theft, etc.

TTB P 5130.005 (09/2007)

Daily Summary Records:

The following types of daily summary records must be maintained:

- Beer bottled;
- Beer racked;
- Beer removed for consumption or sale;
- Beer returned;
- Beer returned after removal from another brewery owned by brewer;
- Brewing materials, beer in process and finished beer on hand;
- Beer tax determined for use at tavern.

Other Records:

Other records that must be kept include:

- Fill tests;
- Ballings;
- Alcohol content;
- Record of unsalable beer.

Other Recordkeeping Matters:

Time of making entries: At the time of operations, or, if posted from source records, no later than the third business day following the operation.

Record retention: Returns, reports and records, including source records, must be kept for three years from date of last entry.

Data Processing: Data maintained on data processing equipment may be kept at the brewery or at another location, if the original operation or transaction source records are kept available for inspection at the brewery.

Photographic copies of records: Reproduced records may be treated as original documents for examination, with the exception of Certificate of Label Approval.

Notice File: A complete and current Notice file must be maintained, readily available at the brewery for inspection.

Brewing Log
27 CFR 25.292

This log serves as the "recipe" for a particular batch of beer. Included is information on materials used, which is recorded on the monthly report in Part 3, and the volume of beer produced, which is recorded on Line 2 (b).

Racking/Bottling Log
27 CFR 25.292

This log is a summary of the racking and bottling activities for the month. An entry is made for each date racking or bottling took place, including the number of barrels that were transferred to racking/bottling, the number of barrels racked/bottled and the barrels lost. It is further broken down by flavor and totaled at the bottom. It is the totals of Barrels to Racking/Bottling, Barrels Racked/Bottled and Losses that need to be included in the monthly report on Lines 6, 9, 10, 22, 23 and 30.

Tax Determined for Use in Tavern Log
27 CFR 25.25 & 25.292

This is a record of beer that is tax determined for use in a tavern on brewery premises. Whenever beer is transferred to a tax-determined tank, the volume must be recorded. Tax-determined tanks must be equipped with an appropriate measuring devise and be marked "tax-determination tank". The monthly total must be reported on Line 15 of the monthly report and included with other removals on the excise tax return.

Daily Shipping Report
27 CFR 25.292

This log is a summary of removals from the brewery, divided by tax period. It also serves as a record of tax determination. Each invoice is listed by date, quantity, type of package and barrels. The barrels removed are totaled at the bottom, separated into kegs and cases. The total barrels removed are multiplied by the appropriate tax rate, in this case $7.00, to determine the tax due for this period. The sum of the barrels removed for both tax periods for the month is entered on the monthly report in Line 14 (d) and (f).

Daily Returned and Daily Destroyed Logs
27 CFR 25.292

These logs record beer returned to the brewery after removal and beer destroyed at the brewery. Totals for the month are entered on the monthly report on Line 7 (d) and (f) for Returns and Line 28 for Destructions.

TTB P 5130.005 (09/2007)

ATF F 5130.9   BREWER'S REPORT OF OPERATIONS

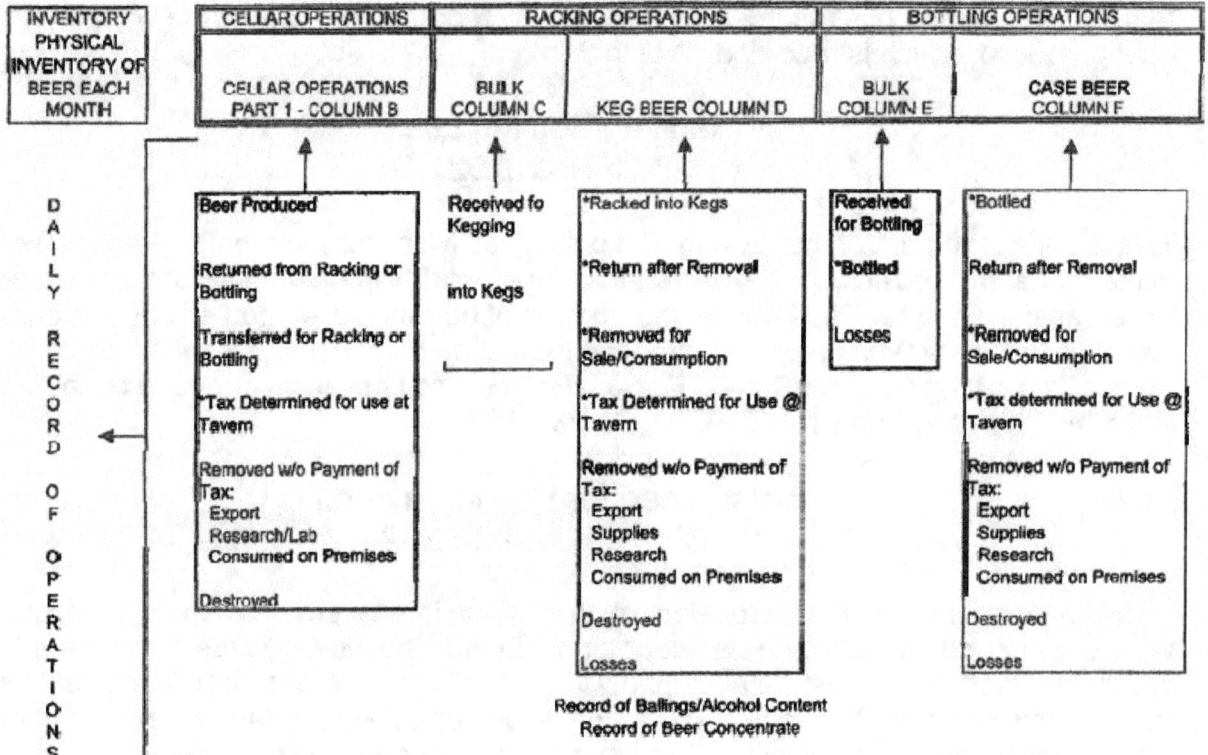

INVENTORY PHYSICAL INVENTORY OF BEER EACH MONTH	CELLAR OPERATIONS		RACKING OPERATIONS		BOTTLING OPERATIONS	
	CELLAR OPERATIONS PART 1 - COLUMN B	BULK COLUMN C	KEG BEER COLUMN D		BULK COLUMN E	CASE BEER COLUMN F

DAILY RECORD OF OPERATIONS

Beer Produced

Returned from Racking or Bottling

Transferred for Racking or Bottling

*Tax Determined for use at Tavern

Removed w/o Payment of Tax:
  Export
  Research/Lab
  Consumed on Premises

Destroyed

Received fo Kegging

into Kegs

*Racked into Kegs

*Return after Removal

*Removed for Sale/Consumption

*Tax Determined for Use @ Tavern

Removed w/o Payment of Tax:
  Export
  Supplies
  Research
  Consumed on Premises

Destroyed

Losses

Received for Bottling

*Bottled

Losses

*Bottled

Return after Removal

*Removed for Sale/Consumption

*Tax determined for Use @ Tavern

Removed w/o Payment of Tax:
  Export
  Supplies
  Research
  Consumed on Premises

Destroyed

Losses

Record of Baffings/Alcohol Content
Record of Beer Concentrate

*Record Summarized on Daily Basis

27 CFR 25.292(a)(2)

DATE:	*1/3/2005*
FLAVOR:	*Amber*
BATCH #:	*1234*
FERMENTER:	*1A*

INGREDIENTS

	Amount Used
Malt 1	*100*
Malt 2	*200*
Wheat	*300*
Hops 1	*100*
Hops 2	*200*
Yeast	*300*
Other	*5*

PROCESS

Calcium Chloride	*XX*
Mash-in	*XX*
Conversion	*XX*
First Wort	*XX*
Calcium Chloride	*XX*
Start Boil, First Hops	*XX*
Dust to LT	*XX*
Floc G	*XX*
End Boil	*XX*
Whilpool Hops	*XX*
Cooling	*XX*

BREW DATA

Kettle Fill Gravity	*12.1*
Kettle Full Volume	*275*
Knock-out Gravity	*13.1*
Rinse Adjustment Volume	*75*
Target Gravity	*10.5*
Final Gravity	*10.4*
Volume Cooled	*300*

COMMENTS

TTB P 5130.005 (09/2007)

Tax Determined for Use in Tavern
27 CFR 25.25(c)(1) & 25.292(a)(8)

Month: January 2005

DATE	TANK	FLAVOR	BARRELS
1/3/2005	1	Raspberry	50.25
1/4/2005	2	Wheat	62.46
1/6/2005	4	Amber	75.32
1/7/2005	3	IPA	47.30
1/10/2005	1	Winter	55.98
1/11/2005	5	Raspberry	67.85
1/13/2005	2	Wheat	63.98
1/14/2005	3	IPA	45.87
1/17/2005	4	Amber	80.42
1/18/2005	1	Winter	57.94
1/19/2005	3	IPA	35.97
1/21/2005	5	Raspberry	56.47
1/24/2005	2	Wheat	47.94
1/27/2005	3	IPA	58.29
1/31/2005	1	Raspberry	45.98
TOTAL			852.02

RACKING LOG
27CFR 25.292 (a)(3), (4), (5), (6)

DATE	BARRELS TO RACKING	BARRELS RACKED	LOSSES	AMBER 1/2	AMBER 1/4	WHEAT 1/2	WHEAT 1/4	RASPBERRY 1/2	RASPBERRY 1/4	WINTER 1/2	WINTER 1/4	IPA 1/2	IPA 1/4
1/3	25.00	25.00	0.00	25.00									
1/4			0.00										
1/5			0.00										
1/6			0.00										
1/7			0.00										
1/10	182.00	180.00	2.00			100.00	80.00						
1/11	75.00	75.00	0.00					75.00					
1/12			0.00										
1/13			0.00										
1/14	5.00	5.00	0.00							5.00			
1/17			0.00										
1/18			0.00										
1/19	55.00	50.00	5.00									50.00	
1/20			0.00										
1/21			0.00										
1/24			0.00										
1/25	100.00	100.00	0.00	75.00	25.00								
1/26			0.00										
1/27			0.00										
1/28	50.00	50.00	0.00										50.00
1/31			0.00										
TOTAL	492.00	485.00	7.00	100.00	25.00	100.00	80.00	75.00	0.00	5.00	0.00	50.00	50.00

BOTTLING LOG
27CFR 25.292 (a)(3), (4), (5), (6)

DATE	BARRELS TO BOTTLING	BARRELS BOTTLED	LOSSES	AMBER 12/12	AMBER 12/24	WHEAT 12/12	WHEAT 12/24	RASPBERRY 12/12	RASPBERRY 12/24	WINTER 12/12	WINTER 12/24	IPA 12/12	IPA 12/24
1/3	101.00	100.02	0.98	100.02									
1/4			0.00										
1/5	252.00	249.97	2.03			174.99	74.98						
1/6			0.00										
1/7			0.00										
1/10	353.00	341.02	11.98			190.01	55.02	95.99					
1/11	203.00	199.99	3.01					199.99					
1/12			0.00										
1/13			0.00										
1/14	526.00	524.97	1.03							199.99	74.98	199.99	50.01
1/17			0.00										
1/18			0.00										
1/19	498.00	474.97	23.03									399.99	74.98
1/20			0.00										
1/21			0.00										
1/24			0.00										
1/25	251.00	250.05	0.95	100.02	50.01	100.02							
1/26			0.00										
1/27			0.00										
1/28	102.00	100.02	1.98									100.02	

TTB P 5130.005 (09/2007)

Daily Shipping Report
27CFR 25.292 (a)(8)
Tax Period: 2005-1

DATE	INVOICE	QUANTITY	KEG	BBLS	CASE	BBLS	TAX
1/3/2005	12489	84	1/2	42			
1/3/2005	12489	40	1/4	10			
1/3/2005	12489	3196			12/12	115.98284	
1/3/2005	12489	372			12/24	26.99976	
1/4/2005	12490	40	1/2	20			
1/4/2005	12490	136	1/4	34			
1/4/2005	12490	1752			12/12	63.58008	
1/4/2005	12490	647			12/24	46.95926	
1/4/2005	45987	2	1/2	1			
1/4/2005	45988	1500			12/12	54.43500	
1/5/2005	12491	92	1/2	46			
1/5/2005	12491	80	1/4	20			
1/5/2005	12491	3361			12/12	121.97069	
1/5/2005	12491	621			12/24	45.07218	
1/6/2005	12492	132	1/2	66			
1/6/2005	12492	76	1/4	19			
1/6/2005	12492	2811			12/12	102.01119	
1/6/2005	12492	656			12/24	47.61248	
1/7/2005	12493	50	1/2	25			
1/7/2005	12493	90	1/4	22.5			
1/7/2005	12493	5000			12/12	181.45000	
1/7/2005	12493	300			12/24	21.77400	
1/7/2005	45989	4	1/2	2			
1/7/2005	45989	6	1/4	1.5			
1/7/2005	45989	236			12/12	8.56444	
1/7/2005	45989	72			12/24	5.22576	
1/10/2005	12494	56	1/2	28			
1/10/2005	12494	84	1/4	21			
1/10/2005	12494	3609			12/12	130.97061	
1/10/2005	12494	827			12/24	60.02366	
1/11/2005	12495	100	1/2	50			
1/11/2005	12495	80	1/4	20			
1/11/2005	12495	3941			12/12	143.01889	
1/11/2005	12495	661			12/24	47.97538	
1/12/2005	12496	72	1/2	36			
1/12/2005	12496	92	1/4	23			
1/12/2005	12496	6007			12/12	217.99403	
1/12/2005	12496	620			12/24	44.99960	
1/13/2005	12497	94	1/2	47			
1/13/2005	12497	64	1/4	16			
1/13/2005	12497	2590			12/12	93.99110	
1/13/2005	12497	730			12/24	52.98340	
1/14/2005	45990	56	1/2	28			
1/14/2005	45990	100	1/4	25			
1/14/2005	45990	2755			12/12	99.97895	
1/14/2005	45990	207			12/24	15.02406	
TOTAL				603		1748.59736	$16,461.20

Daily Shipping Report							
Tax Period: 2005-2							
DATE	**INVOICE**	**QUANTITY**	**KEG**	**BBLS**	**CASE**	**BBLS**	**TAX**
1/17/2005	12498	58	1/2	29			
1/17/2005	12498	132	1/4	33			
1/17/2005	12498	5539			12/12	201.01031	
1/17/2005	12498	592			12/24	42.96736	
1/18/2005	12499	118	1/2	59			
1/18/2005	12499	24	1/4	6			
1/18/2005	12499	3830			12/12	138.99070	
1/18/2005	12499	648			12/24	47.03184	
1/19/2005	45991	88	1/2	44			
1/19/2005	45991	64	1/4	16			
1/19/2005	45991	1957			12/12	71.01953	
1/19/2005	45991	399			12/24	28.95942	
1/20/2005	12500	52	1/2	26			
1/20/2005	12500	124	1/4	31			
1/20/2005	12500	5732			12/12	208.01428	
1/20/2005	12500	468			12/24	33.96744	
1/21/2005	12501	74	1/2	37			
1/21/2005	12501	96	1/4	24			
1/21/2005	12501	3774			12/12	136.95846	
1/21/2005	12501	772			12/24	56.03176	
1/24/2005	45992	94	1/2	47			
1/24/2005	45992	76	1/4	19			
1/24/2005	45992	2177			12/12	79.00333	
1/24/2005	45992	923			12/24	66.99134	
1/25/2005	12502	100	1/2	50			
1/25/2005	12502	68	1/4	17			
1/25/2005	12502	3913			12/12	142.00277	
1/25/2005	12502	317			12/24	23.00786	
1/26/2005	12503	54	1/2	27			
1/26/2005	12503	60	1/4	15			
1/26/2005	12503	3003			12/12	108.97887	
1/26/2005	12503	951			12/24	69.02358	
1/27/2005	12504	66	1/2	33			
1/27/2005	12504	96	1/4	24			
1/27/2005	12504	1461			12/12	53.01969	
1/27/2005	12504	220			12/24	15.96760	
1/28/2005	12505	106	1/2	53			
1/28/2005	12505	148	1/4	37			
1/28/2005	12505	6007			12/12	217.99403	
1/28/2005	12505	716			12/24	51.96728	
1/31/2005	12506	68	1/2	34			
1/31/2005	12506	44	1/4	11			
1/31/2005	12506	3554			12/12	128.97466	
1/31/2005	12506	702			12/24	50.95116	
TOTAL				672		1972.83327	$18,513.81

TTB P 5130.005 (09/2007)

DAILY RETURNED LOG
27 CFR 25.292 (a)(12)

DATE	DESCRIPTION	SIZE	QUANTITY	BARRELS	REASON	REMOVED BY
1/3/2005	Amber	1/2	10	5	bad date	JG
1/10/2005	Raspberry	12/24	96	6.97	bad date	PH
1/12/2005	Wheat	1/4	24	6	bad date	JG
1/19/2005	Winter	12/24	140	10.16	damaged packaging	SH
1/26/2005	Amber	12/24	56	4.06	bad date	PH

DAILY DESTROYED LOG
27 CFR 25.292 (a)(14)

DATE	DESCRIPTION	SIZE	QUANTITY	BARRELS	REASON	REMOVED BY
1/3/2005	Amber	1/2	10	5	bad date	JG
1/5/2005	IPA	1/2	4	2	leaking	SH
1/10/2005	Raspberry	12/24	96	6.97	bad date	PH
1/12/2005	Wheat	1/4	24	6	bad date	JG
1/19/2005	Winter	12/24	140	10.16	damaged packaging	SH
1/26/2005	Amber	12/24	56	4.06	bad date	PH
1/28/2005	Wheat	1/4	4	1	leaking	SH

TTB P 5130.005 (09/2007)

Inventory

A formal inventory must be taken at least once a month, within 7 days of the end of the month. This inventory needs to show:

1) The date inventory was taken;
2) The quantity of beer;
3) Any losses, gains and shortages uncovered since the last inventory;
4) Signature under penalties of perjury.

| | Bay 1 | | | | Bay 2 | | | | Bay 3 | | | | Bay 4 | | | | Bay 5 | | | | Bay 6 | | | |
| | Amber | | | | Wheat | | | | Raspberry | | | | Winter | | | | IPA | | | | | | | |
	1/2	1/4	12/12	12/24	1/2	1/4	12/12	12/24	1/2	1/4	12/12	12/24	1/2	1/4	12/12	12/24	1/2	1/4	12/12	12/24	1/2	1/4	12/12	12/24
Count			304	414			7303	703			303	110			28	138			10637	634				
Barrels	0	0	11.03	30.05	0	0	265.03	51.02	0	0	11	7.98	0	0	1.02	10.02	0	0	386.02	46.02	0	0	0	0

| | TOTAL | | | | | Bay 7 | | | |
	1/2	1/4	12/12	12/24		1/2	1/4	12/12	12/24
Count	366	596	18575	1999	Count				
Barrels	183	149	674.09	145.09	Barrels	0	0	0	0

| | Bay 13 | | | | Bay 12 | | | | Bay 11 | | | | Bay 10 | | | | Bay 9 | | | | Bay 8 | | | |
| | Amber | | | | Wheat | | | | Raspberry | | | | Winter | | | | IPA | | | | | | | |
	1/2	1/4	12/12	12/24	1/2	1/4	12/12	12/24	1/2	1/4	12/12	12/24	1/2	1/4	12/12	12/24	1/2	1/4	12/12	12/24	1/2	1/4	12/12	12/24
Count	116	120			188	188			32	0			12	104			18	184						
Barrels	58	30	0	0	94	47	0	0	16	0	0	0	6	26	0	0	9	46	0	0	0	0	0	0

I declare under the penalties of perjury that this inventory, including the documents submitted in support thereof, has been examined by me and, to the best of my knowledge and belief, is true, correct and complete.

DATE TAKEN:_____   TAKEN BY:_____

TTB P 5130.005 (09/2007)

INVENTORY RECONCILIATION
JANUARY 31, 2005
27 CFR 25.294

BEER IN KEGS	1/2	1/4	**TOTAL BARRELS**
BEGINNING INVENTORY	690	443	1,133.00
RACKED	330	155	485.00
REMOVALS	830	445	1,275.00
DESTROYED BEER	7	7	14.00
ENDING INVENTORY BALANCE	183	149	332.00
LOSS/(GAIN) TO INVENTORY	-	(3)	(3.00)

BEER IN BOTTLES	12/12	12/24	**TOTAL BARRELS**
BEGINNING INVENTORY	1,633.91	681.30	2,315.21
BOTTLED	1,861.03	379.98	2,241.01
REMOVALS	2,820.00	895.00	3,715.00
DESTROYED BEER	-	21.19	21.19
ENDING INVENTORY BALANCE	674.09	145.09	819.18
LOSS/(GAIN) TO INVENTORY	0.85	-	0.85

I declare under the penalties of perjury that this inventory, including the documents submitted in support thereof, has been examined by me and, to the best of my knowledge and belief, is true, correct and complete.

TAKEN BY:

DATE TAKEN: _____   _____

Form 5130.9, Brewer's Report of Operations
27 CFR 25.297

Who Must Use this Report:

The Brewer's Report of Operations needs to be used if you produce more than 5000 barrels per year or you bottle or keg your beer.

The Heading:

- Write in your Employer Identification Number (EIN) at the top of the page.
- Enter your Brewery Number, in the following format: BR-ST-AAA-### where ST is your state abbreviation, AAA is the approved abbreviation of the company name and ### is a one to five digit number.
- Enter the name of the brewery as shown on your Brewer's Notice, address and telephone number.
- Indicate the year and month or quarter the report covers.

Part 1 – Beer Summary:

- On Line 1 in each column, enter the "On hand end of period" figure from Line 33 of the previous report.
- Lines 2 through 13 are activities that add to your beer inventory.
- Lines 14 through 31 are activities that decrease your beer inventory.
- Row totals are entered in Column G.
- See samples for more specific instructions.

Part 2 – Report Period Tax Payments:

Enter information on all tax returns completed for the report period.

Part 3 – Summary of Materials Used and Wort Produced:

Show use of materials for beer making.

Part 4 – Cereal Beverage Summary:

Show production of cereal beverage, if any.

TTB P 5130.005 (09/2007)

Part 5 – Remarks:

Use this space to explain any unusual transactions.

Signature: The person signing the form must have Power of Attorney or Signing Authority.

Filing Dates:

The Report Form 5130.9 is due 15 days after the close of the period, i.e. by the 15th of the next month if filing monthly or the 15th of the month following the quarter if filing quarterly.

Eligibility for Filing Quarterly Report:

You are eligible to file quarterly if you produce less than 10,000 barrels per year. In this instance, production includes beer produced, water added in cellars and beer received from other brewers for the previous year. In order to begin filing quarterly, state this in the remarks section of your last monthly report before filing quarterly, or your first report if you are just beginning production.

How to File:

The Brewer's Report of Operations may now be filed in two ways: via mail with the paper form or electronically with pay.gov. Pay.gov allows brewers to complete and submit reports and excise tax returns online. The electronic form is completed in the same manner as the manual form, but provides certain checks to help ensure the form is completed correctly. Prior registration is required before using pay.gov.

DEPARTMENT OF THE TREASURY
BUREAU OF ALCOHOL, TOBACCO AND FIREARMS

BREWER'S REPORT OF OPERATIONS

(You must follow the instructions on the back of this report)

Our Brewery EIN is:
12-3456789

Our Brewery Number is:
BR-ST-AAA-###

ATF can reach us by telephone at:
(503) 123-4567

What is your brewery's name? **ABC Brewing**

What is the location of your brewery?

123 NE Main St.	Portland	Multnomah	OR	97654
(Number and Street)	(City)	(County)	(State)	(Zip Code)

Reporting Period (Enter Year) **2005**

Monthly Report for (Enter Month) **January**   OR

(See Instruction 3.)

Quarterly Report for
☐ January - March   ☐ July - September
☐ April - June   ☐ October - December

Part 1 - Beer Summary (Barrels)

Operations (a)		Cellar (b)	Racking Bulk (c)	Racking Keg (d)	Bottling (e)	Bottling Case (f)	Totals (g)
Additions to beer inventory (round your entries to the nearest second decimal)							
1. On hand beginning of this report period	(1)	3225.00	0.00	1133.00	0.00	2315.21	6673.21
2. We produced by fermentation	(2)	2000.00					2000.00
3. We added water and other liquids in cellar operations							0.00
4. Beer received from racking and bottling							0.00
5. Beer received from other brewers							0.00
6. Beer received from cellars	(3)		492.00		2286.00		2778.00
7. Beer returned to our brewery	(4)			11.00		21.19	32.19
8. Beer received from another brewery							0.00
9. Racked	(5)			485.00			485.00
10. Bottled	(6)					2241.01	2241.01
11. Physical inventory disclosed an overage	(7)			3.00			3.00
12.							0.00
13. Total additions to beer inventory	(8)	5225.00	492.00	1632.00	2286.00	4577.41	14212.41
Removals from beer inventory (round your entries to the nearest second decimal)							
14. Removed for consumption or sale	(9)			1275.00		3721.43	4996.43
15. Tax determined for use at tavern on brewery prem	(10)	852.02					852.02
16. Removed without payment of tax for export							0.00
17. Removed without payment of tax as supplies (vessels, etc.)							0.00
18. Removed without payment of tax for use in research or							0.00
19. Removed without payment of tax to other breweries and pilot brewing plants							0.00
20. Beer unfit for sale removed for use in manufacturing							0.00
21. Beer consumed on premises							0.00
22. Beer transferred for racking	(11)	492.00					492.00
23. Beer transferred for bottling	(12)	2286.00					2286.00
24. Beer returned to cellars							0.00
25. Beer racked	(13)		485.00				485.00
26. Beer bottled	(14)				2241.00		2241.00
27. Laboratory samples							0.00
28. Beer destroyed at brewery	(15)			14.00		21.19	35.19
29. Beer transferred to a distilled spirits plant							0.00
30. Recorded losses, including theft	(16)		7.00		45.00		52.00
31. Physical inventory disclosed a shortage	(17)					0.85	0.85
32.							0.00
33. On hand end of period	(18)	1594.98	0.00	343.00	0.00	833.94	2771.92
34. Total beer	(19)	5225.00	492.00	1632.00	2286.00	4577.41	14212.41

ATF F 5130.9 (8-2001) Previous edition is obsolete.

TTB P 5130.005 (09/2007)

35. Additions to beer inventory	(+)	(-)	36. Removals from beer inventory	(+)	(-)

Under penalties of perjury I declare that this report is supported by true, complete, and correct records that are available for inspection at my brewery. I have examined this report and to the best of my knowledge and belief it is true, complete, and correct.

John Smith	Owner	2/12/2005
Signature	Title	Date

Part 2 – Report Period Tax Payments (See Instructions – Part 2)

	Return Serial Number	Date Filed	Tax Liability	Adjustments	Amount Paid
(20)	2005-1	1/27/2005	$16,504.00	$45.00	$16,549.00
	2005-2	2/12/2005	$10,803.00	-$85.75	$10,717.25
			$	$	$
			$	$	$
			$	$	$
			$	$	$
			$	$	$

Part 3 – Summary of Materials Used and Wort Produced

Item	Hops (pounds) (a)	Hops Extract (pounds) (b)	Hops Equivalent (c)	Wort (barrels) (d)	Malted Barley (e)	specify (f)	specify (g)	specify (h)
1. Material for beer & cereal beverage	(21) 4076				241,594			
2. Wort received and used								
3. Wort removed								
4.								

Part 4 – Cereal Beverage Summary (products at less than 0.5% alcohol by volume)

1. Produced	Bbls.	5.			Bbls.
2. Removed	Bbls.	6.			Bbls.
3. Loss and wastage	Bbls.	7.			Bbls.
4. Received from DSP	Bbls.	8. On hand end of period			Bbls.

Part 5 – Remarks

Instructions

This is the Brewer's Report of Operations. You must file this report if:

- ☒ You produce more than 5,000 barrels of beer per year or
- ☒ You produce not more than 5,000 barrels of beer per year and you bottle or keg your beer.

1. Where can I get help for this report? You may call us toll-free at (866) 345-2282.

2. Where do I file this report? Make an original and a copy.

Send original to us at this address:
Chief, National Revenue Center
Bureau of Alcohol, Tobacco and Firearms
550 Main Street, Room 8002
Cincinnati, Ohio 45202-3263

☒ You must keep a copy at the brewery available for inspection by ATF officers.

3. When must I file this report? You must file this report by the fifteenth day after the end of the reporting period.

4. What is the reporting period? File this report for the following report periods:

If you....	Then the reporting period is....
Produce more than 10,000 barrels per year	Monthly – enter the month you are reporting
Produce not more than 10,000 barrels per year	Quarterly – by calendar quarters – check the box for the quarter you are reporting
Discontinuing business	Monthly – for the months in the final quarter you are in business – enter the month you are reporting. Write "final report" in Part 5 – Remarks.

Part 1 – Cellar Operations

5. How do I report beer on this form? You must report beer in barrels. One barrel is 31 gallons. Round your entries to the nearest second decimal place.

6. I adjusted a previous period tax return. Now, how do I report adjustments on this report? If you adjusted an Excise Tax Return (ATF F 5000.24) and the adjustment affects the quantity of beer you previously reported on your Brewer's Report of Operations then you must record an adjustment on this report to correct the error.

Follow these instructions:
- ☒ Make these adjustments on lines 35 and 36, in the plus or minus columns as appropriate (additions on line 35, removals on line 36).
- ☒ Do not include these adjustments in the totals on lines 13 or 34.
- ☒ Explain your adjusting entries in Part 5 – Remarks. Attach additional pages if necessary.

7. I have a shortage to report on Part 1. Must I explain? You must explain any shortage you report in Part 1. Give your explanation in Part 5 – Remarks, or in a separate statement signed by you under penalty of perjury. We may assess the tax on shortages if we are not satisfied that your explanation is sufficient to relieve the tax liability.

8. Where do I report destruction of tax determined beer? When you destroy beer after tax determination for use at your tavern, report in this way: first, list the beer as a return to the brewery on line 7; then, report the destruction on line 28.

ATF F 5130.9 (8-2001)

Beer Materials

Why do we care?
1. We reported it on the Beer Statistical Release.
2. States use the data for crop projections.
3. It is a good way to determine if the company is reporting correctly.
   a. Yields should be around 2-6 pounds of grain per barrel of beer.
   b. Large volumes of materials and small amounts of beer show potential lost tax revenues.
4. Ensure the product doesn't include unacceptable ingredients.

What material information do we report on the Statistical Release?
1. Barley and barley products
2. Corn and corn products
3. Hops (dry)
4. Hops (used as extracts)
5. Malt and malt products
6. Rice and rice products
7. Sugar and syrups
8. Wheat and wheat products
9. Other

What about Flavoring and Other products?
1. We determine the category by how they use the material.
   a. Example: You put a lemonade syrup used to make the final product lemon flavored in flavor. However, you put the same syrup used to increase the sugar content of the final product in sugar.
2. We report flavors in the Other category on the release
3. Only put it in other if everything else has been tried.

Materials List
1. It defines categories for materials.
2. It is a subset of a much larger list
3. If it isn't on the list, please call/email me and ask.

TTB P 5130.005 (09/2007)

1. MALT AND MALT PRODUCTS

- 2-ROW
- ACIDULATED
- ALBA
- AMBER
- AMBER MALT
- BLACK
- BLACK MALT
- BROWN
- CARA AROMA
- CARA BROWN
- CARA FA SPECIAL
- CARA M AMBER
- CARA MALT
- CARA PIL
- CARA RED
- CARAMEL
- CARAMEL (CARA PILS)
- CHOC
- CHOCOLATE
- CRAFT
- CRYSTAL
- CRYSTAL DARK
- DARK MUNICH
- DUNKEL
- GOLDEN PROMISE
- HALCYON
- HELL
- HOEPFNER
- JOE WHITE
- K.K. MALT
- LIGHT MUNICH
- MARIS OTTER
- MELANOIDIN
- MELLO
- MUNICH
- PALE
- PALE RYE
- PILSNER
- PIPKIN
- ROAST MALT
- ROASTED MALT
- SMOKED
- SPECIAL MALT
- SPECIALTY
- SPROUTS
- TRADITIONAL ALE
- VIENNA
- WEIZEN
- WEYERMANN

2. CORN AND CORN PRODUCTS

- AMIDEX
- BREWERS FLAKES
- BREWERS GRITS
- CERALINE
- CEREALS
- CORALLINE
- CORN
- CORN FLAKES
- CORN GRITS
- CREAM MEAL
- GALEX
- GRITS
- GRITS (YELLOW/WHITE)
- GRITS GELATINE
- JIFFY MALT
- JIFFY MALT BREWERS FLAKES
- JIFFY MALT FLAKES
- MAIZE
- MEAL
- PEARL STARCH
- REFINED GRITS
- SHAKER
- STARCH (From Coors brewery)

3. RICE AND RICE PRODUCTS

- RICE
- RICE FLAKES
- RICE MEAL

4. WHEAT AND WHEAT PRODUCTS

- ALCOMEAL
- BRU-WHEAT
- FARINA
- FLOUR
- FREMAL (BARLEY PRO)
- GOLDEN GRITS
- MALTOID (WHEAT FLAKES)
- PROMALT
- WARTEX
- WHEAT GRITS
- WHEATOSE

5. BARLEY AND BARLEY PRODUCTS
BARLEY
BARLEY FLAKES
BARLEY GRITS
BARLEY MALT
BARLYNE
BLACK BARLEY
BREW MEAL
BREWERS AID
BREWERS AID GROUND
FORMAL MALT
FROMALT
PEARL BARLEY
PERFECTION BARLEY
STARNCO GRITS

6. SORGHUM GRAIN AND SORGHUM GRAIN PRODUCTS
KAFFAR (KAFFIR)
MARIZONE
MELLO GRITS
MILO
MILO GRITS
MILO MAIZE
TEX-O-MALT

7. HOPS
DRIHOPS
HOPS
PELLETS

8. HOP EXTRACTS
CANICO
HOP CONCENTRATE
HOP EXTENDER
HOPESO
HOPTONE
HOPUION
LUPULON
MALTECON
ULMAKIN

9. HOP EXTRACT EQUIVALENT
(POUNDS)

10. SUGAR AND SYRUPS
ACME NO. 70 (CORN SUGAR)
ALCOSE
AMAIZE
ARGO
BEET SUGAR SYRUP
BODEXT SYRUP
BODY SUGAR
BODY SYRUP

BRAVO SYRUP
BREW SUGAR
BRUTOSE
CANE SUGAR
CANE SUGAR RESIDUE
CEROLOSE SUGAR (DEXTROSI
CLEARBREW
CORN EXTRACT
CORN SUGAR
CORN SYRUP
CORN SYRUP SOLIDS
CREAMALT
DEXTORA
DEXTROSE
DIACO
DIAMALT
DIASTATICE MALT
DRYDOX CORN SUGAR
EMKA MALT
F.L. SYRUP
F.M. SYRUP
GLUCOSE SUGAR
GRANULATED SUGAR
HAMKE
HAMMERSLAG
HAURMALT
HELBERG SYRUP
HFCS
HIGH FRUCTOSE CORN SYRUP
HONEY
HYDREX SYRUP
INVERTOSE
K.K. DEXTRINE
K.K. DEXTRINE MALT
KOSS SYRUP
LIQUID ADJUNCT
LIQUID CORN
LIQUID DEXTROSE
LODEX
LOVUDEX
MALCO SYRUP
MALDEX
MALT EXTRACT
MALT EXTRACT SYRUP
MALT FREE QUOTA SYRUP
MALT SYRUP
MALTO-DEXTRINE
MALTOSE SUGAR
MAPLE SYRUP
MANIOCA SYRUP
MAZAN
MAZEREX

TTB P 5130.005 (09/2007)

MELLO
MOLASSES
NECTORAL
NECTROSE
NEUDEX
NEUDEX SYRUP
NO. 12
NULOMOLINE
PACEX
PALE MELLO
PERFECTO
PNMOSE
QUOTE FREE SYRUP
REFINERS SYRUP
SPECIAL BREWING SYRUP
SUCREME
SUGAR
SWECTOSE
SYRUP SOLUTION
SYRUP(S)
TEMPOENE
WAVERYLY

11. FLAVORING PRODUCTS
(GALLONS/POUNDS)

12. OTHER
ANY OTHER MATERIALS NOT LISTEI
ABOVE THAT ARE EXTRACTED AND
ALCOHOL PRODUCING FOR
EXAMPLE:
CUBAN SWEET POTATOES
IDA GRITS
MAMIOCA
MANDIOCA MEAL
POTATO DEXTRINE
POTATO FLOUR
POTATO POWDER
POTATO STARCH
TAPIOCA
UNREFINED GRANULAR
TAPIOCA

Explanation of Entries on Sample "Brewer's Report of Operations"

1.   These figures are carried forward from Line 33 of the previous report.

2.   The brewer produced 2,000 barrels by fermentation. Note: Part 3 on the reverse needs to indicate amount of materials used to produce this beer.

3.   The brewer removed 492 barrels of bulk beer to be racked and 2,286 barrels to be bottled. Note Items 10 and 11 below.

        The brewer had 11 barrels of kegged and 21.19 barrels of cased beer returned to the brewery.

5.   The brewer racked 485 barrels of beer. This figure must match Line 25, Column (c). See Item 12, below.

6.   The brewer bottled 2,241.01 barrels of beer. This figure must match Line 26, Column (e). See Item 13, below.

7.   The brewer noted an overage of 3 barrels of kegged beer in the monthly inventory.

8.   Total Lines 1 through 12 for each column in Line 13. This represents the total quantity to be accounted for in the month and should agree with the figures in Line 34.

        The brewer removed for consumption 1,275 barrels of kegged beer and 3,721.43 barrels of cased beer. This includes sales to distributors, employees, dock sales, charitable contributions and any other taxable removal.

10.   Brewer tax-determined 852.02 barrels of beer for use in the tavern on brewery premises.

11.   Brewer transferred 492 barrels of bulk beer from cellar operations to racking operations. This figure must match Line 6, Column (c). See Item 3, above.

12.   Brewer transferred 2286 barrels of bulk beer from cellar operations to bottling operations. This figure must match Line 6, Column (e). See Item 3, above.

3.   Brewer racked 485 barrels of beer. This figure must match Line 9, Column (d). See Item 4, above.

4.   Brewer bottled 2,241 barrels of beer. This figure must match Line 10, Column (f). See Item 5, above.

5.   The brewer destroyed 14 barrels of kegged and 21.19 barrels of cased beer.

TTB P 5130.005 (09/2007)

Explanation of Entries on Sample "Brewer's Report of Operations"

16.   Brewer recorded a loss of 7 barrels in racking and 45 barrels in bottling. Explain any unusual losses in Part 5 – Remarks.

17.   The monthly inventory showed a shortage of 24 barrels in kegged beer. Shortages must either be properly explained or taxpaid.

18.   Line 33 equals Line 13 minus Lines 14 through 32. This represents the amount of beer on hand at the end of the reporting period. These figures will be transferred to Line 1 on the next report.

19.   Line 34 is the sum of Line 14 through 33. The figures on Line 34 must match the figures on Line 13.

20.   The brewer recorded the serial number, date filed, tax liability, adjustments and amount paid for each tax return for the month covered by the report.

21.   The brewer used 4,076 pounds of hops and 241,594 pound of malted barley in production.

Reconciliation Report of Operations to Tax Returns
Jan-05

Report of Operations

Removed for Consumption or Sale (bbls)		Tax Rate	Total Tax
Kegs	1275		
Cases	3721.43		
Tavern	852.02		
	5848.45	7.00	40939.15
Less Returns as Offsets			
Cases	32.19	7.00	225.33
			40,713.82

Tax Returns

S/N 2005-1	19,618.48
S/N 2005-2	21,095.34
	40,713.82

Note:

Adjustments to tax Liability are a separate matter

TTB P 5130.005 (09/2007)

Part 1 - Beer Summary (Barrels)

Operations	Cellar	Racking		Bottling		Totals
		Bulk	Keg	Bulk	Case	
(a)	(b)	(c)	(d)	(e)	(f)	(g)
Additions to beer inventory (round your entries to the nearest second decimal)						
. On hand beginning of this report period	**ON HAND FROM PREVIOUS REPORT #1**					
We produced by fermentation	#11					
We added water and other liquids in cellar operations	#11					
. Beer received from racking and bottling	#2					
Beer received from other brewers						
. Beer received from cellars		#3				
Beer returned to our brewery						
. Beer received from another brewery						
. Racked			#5			
0. Bottled					#6	
1. Physical inventory disclosed an overage						
2.						
13. Total additions to beer inventory	#7					
Removals from beer inventory (round your entries to the nearest second decimal)						
14. Removed for consumption or sale			#9 *Verify against Tax Return		#3 *Verify against Tax Return	
15. Tax determined for use at tavern on brewery premises	#8 *					
16. Removed without payment of tax for export	#9 ^		#9 ^Beer for Export 1689's		#9 ^Beer for Export 1689's	
17. Removed without payment of tax as supplies (vessels, etc.)						
8. Removed without payment of tax for use in research or testing						
9. Removed without payment of tax to other breweries and not brewing plants						
0. Beer unfit for sale removed for use in manufacturing						
1. Beer consumed on premises						
22. Beer transferred for racking	#3					
23. Beer transferred for bottling						
4. Beer returned to cellars		#2		#2		
5. Beer racked		#5				
6. Beer bottled				#6		
7. Laboratory samples						
8. Beer destroyed at brewery						
9. Beer transferred to a distilled spirits plant						
0. Recorded losses, including theft						
31. Physical inventory disclosed a shortage			#10		#10	
2.						
33. On hand end of period	**Transferred to Next Report**					
34. Total beer	#7					

Helpful Hints in Preparing Form 5130.9, Brewer's Report of Operations

1. **Check that Line 1, Part** 1, agrees with Line 33, Part 1, of the previous month's report. On hand end of month **should equal on** hand beginning of month. The first report filed should have zero on hand.

2. Check that Line 3, Column (b), Part 1 agrees with Line 20 Part 1 column and equals the amount in column (c).

3. Check that Line 6, Column (c), Part 1, agrees with Line 22, Column (b).

4. [illegible]

5. Check that Line 9, Column (d), Part 1, agrees with Line 25, Column (c), Part 1.

6. Check that Line 10, Column (f), Part 1, agrees with line 26, Column (e) Part 1.

7. Check that Line 13 and 34, Part 1, are mathematically correct and agree with each other. The figures in these two lines should be the same in all columns.

8. Check that the quantities reported on Line 14 and/or 15, Part 1 minus the quantity shown on Line 7, Part 1, agree with the total Tax Liability (Line 17) on the tax returns filed for the month.

9. If any beer is exported without payment of tax, the quantities reported on Line 16 & 17 Part 1 must equal the amount of barrels totaled on all Forms 1689, Beer for Exportation, for the month.

10. Check that shortages reported on Line 31, Columns (d) and (f), Part 1, are either properly explained and/or taxpaid.

11. If there are entries in Part 1, Line 2 and 3 or Part 4, Line 1, there should be entries in Part 3. When any beer or cereal beverages are produced the brewer must account for any products used in the production process. IE: 10 pounds of malt used, 50 hops used, etc. **This is reported in Part 3,** Summary of Materials Used and Wort Produced.

12. Please be sure that someone who has the authority to do so signs the monthly report and tax returns.

TTB P 5130.005 (09/2007)

Common Problems Found On The Brewer's Report of Operations
ATF F 5130.9 (revised 8-2001)-all previous editions are obsolete

The actual ATF forms must be used. "Home made" or computer-generated forms are not permitted unless a variance has been requested and granted.

- Do not use negative numbers on this form.
- If you need to make a correction to a previously filed report, you must clearly mark the top of the new report as "AMENDED".
- The reports must be filed timely even if no activity occurred at the brewery during the reporting period.
- All reporting is done in barrels (not gallons), unless otherwise noted. An example of an exception is in the "Summary of Materials Used", where some items are reported in pounds.
- The individual signing the report must have signing authority or a Power of Attorney on file with the National Revenue Center.
- ***Who may use the Brewer's Report of Operations?*** Any approved brewery or brewpub may use this form, but if you produce more than 5,000 barrels of beer per year or bottle or keg you beer for removal from your premises you *must* use this form.
- Line 15 "Beer tax determined for use in the tavern on brewery premise: is for the beer that is sold and served on the brewery premise. Tax is due on beer shown on this line.
- Line 21 "Beer consumed on premise" is only for the beer that is served on premise without a charge. For example, beer that is served in a tasting room after a tour and there is no charge of any type to the customer for the beer or the tour. No tax is due on beer shown on this line.
- Each line on the form of the form has a total column in column (g). Column (g) must be filled in if there is an entry on that line.
- Each column has a total line on Line 13 "Total additions to beer inventory" and Line 34 "Total beer". The appropriate column must be filled in on line 13, or if there is an entry in the column for removals, the appropriate block must be filled in on line 34.
- Please note that line 13 includes all additions to beer inventory, as well as on hand beginning of period. Line 34 included all removals, as well as on hand end of period.
- The totals on Line 13 must match the totals on Line 34. All beer included in the "Additions to beer inventory" must be accounted for in the "Removals from beer inventory".
- Line 33 "On hand end of period" must match Line 1 "On hand beginning of period" for the following month's/quarter's report.
- Part 3 "Summary of Materials Used and Wort Produced". This is where you will list the materials used to produce your product. They are classified as follows:
  - o Hops in pounds in column (a)
  - o Hops extract in pounds in column (b)
  - o Hops extract equivalent in column (c)
  - o Wort in barrels in column (d)

Specify the following general classifications in pounds in columns (e), (f), (g) and (h) as:
- o Barley products
- o Corn and Corn Products
- o Sugar and Syrups
- o Wheat and Wheat Products
- o Flavoring Products
- o Rice and Rice Products
- o **Sorghum Grain and Sor**ghum Grain Products

TTB P 5130.005 (09/2007)

The actual ATF forms must be used. "Home made" or computer-generated forms are not permitted unless a variance has been requested and granted.

- Do not use negative numbers on this form.
- If you need to make a correction to a previously filed report, you must clearly mark the top of the new report as "AMENDED".
- The reports must be filed timely even if no activity occurred at the brewery during the reporting period.
- All reporting is done in barrels (not gallons), unless otherwise noted. An example of an exception is in the "Summary of Materials Used", where some items are reported in pounds.
- The individual signing the report must have signing authority or a Power of Attorney on file with the National Revenue Center.
- ***Who may use the Brewer's Report of Operations?*** Any approved brewery or brewpub may use this form, but if you produce more than 5,000 barrels of beer per year or bottle or keg you beer for removal from your premises you *must* use this form.
- Line 15 "Beer tax determined for use in the tavern on brewery premise: is for the beer that is sold and served on the brewery premise. Tax is due on beer shown on this line.
- Line 21 "Beer consumed on premise" is only for the beer that is served on premise without a charge. For example, beer that is served in a tasting room after a tour and there is no charge of any type to the customer for the beer or the tour. No tax is due on beer shown on this line.
- Each line on the form of the form has a total column in column (g). Column (g) must be filled in if there is an entry on that line.
- Each column has a total line on Line 13 "Total additions to beer inventory" and Line 34 "Total beer". The appropriate column must be filled in on line 13, or if there is an entry in the column for removals, the appropriate block must be filled in on line 34.
- Please note that line 13 includes all additions to beer inventory, as well as on hand beginning of period. Line 34 included all removals, as well as on hand end of period.
- The totals on Line 13 must match the totals on Line 34. All beer included in the "Additions to beer inventory" must be accounted for in the "Removals from beer inventory".
- Line 33 "On hand end of period" must match Line 1 "On hand beginning of period" for the following month's/quarter's report.
- Part 3 "Summary of Materials Used and Wort Produced". This is where you will list the materials used to produce your product. They are classified as follows:
  - Hops in pounds in column (a)
  - Hops extract in pounds in column (b)
  - Hops extract equivalent in column (c)
  - Wort in barrels in column (d)

Form 5130.26, Brewpub Report of Operations
27 CFR 25.297

Who May Use this Report:

You may use this report if you produce less than 5000 barrels of beer per year and do not bottle or keg your beer.

Heading:

- Write in your Employer Identification Number (EIN) at the top of the page.
- Enter your Brewery Number, in the following format: BR-ST-AAA-### where ST is your state abbreviation, AAA is the approved abbreviation of the company name and ### is a one to five digit number.
- Enter the name of the brewery as shown on your Brewer's Notice, address and telephone number.
- Indicate the year and quarter the report covers.

Part 1 – Cellar Operations:

- The left-hand section shows additions to inventory.
- The right-hand section shows removals from inventory.
- Totals are entered in lines 8 and 17.

Part 2 – Report Period Tax Payments:

Include all tax payments for the quarter covered by the report.

Part 3 – Summary of Materials Used and Wort Produced:

Show use of materials for beer making.

Signature:

The person signing the form must have Power of Attorney or Signing Authority.

Filing Dates:

The Brewpub Report Form 5130.26 is due 15 days after the close of the quarter, i.e. by the 15th of April for the January through March report.

How to File:

The Brewer's Report of Operations may now be filed in two ways: via mail with the paper form or electronically with pay.gov. Pay.gov allows brewers to complete and submit reports and excise tax returns online. The electronic form is completed in the same manner as the manual form, but provides certain checks to help ensure the form is completed correctly.

TTB P 5130.005 (09/2007)

DEPARTMENT OF THE TREASURY
ALCOHOL AND TOBACCO TAX AND TRADE BUREAU (TTB)

BREWPUB REPORT OF OPERATIONS

(You must follow the instructions on the back of this report.)

Our Brewery EIN is:
12-3456789

Our Brewery Number is:
BR-ST-AAA-###

TTB can reach us by telephone at:
(503) 123-4567

What is your brewery's name?
ABC Brewing

What is the location of your brewery?

123 NE Main St.	Portland	Multnomah	OR	97654
(Number and Street)	(City)	(County)	(State)	(Zip Code)

Reporting Period *(Enter year)* 2005
Quarterly Report for

[X] January - March　　[ ] April - June　　[ ] July - September　　[ ] October - December

Part 1 - Cellar Operations

Additions to beer inventory		Number of barrels	Removals from beer inventory		Number of barrels
1. Produced by fermentation	(1)	470.25	10. Beer tax determined for use in the tavern	(5)	466.25
2. We added water and other liquids in cellar operations			11. Beer transferred to other breweries or pilot brewery	(6)	3.75
3. Beer received from other brewers	(2)	2.00	12. Beer consumed on premises		
4. Beer returned to our brewery	(3)	0.50	13. Beer destroyed at brewery	(7)	0.50
5. Physical inventory disclosed an overage			14. Recorded beer losses, including theft (explain in remarks)	(8)	2.25
6.			15. Physical inventory disclosed a shortage (see instruction 5)		
7.			16.		
8. Our total beer to account for is (add rows 1 through 7)	(4)	472.75	17. Total removals from inventory (add rows 10 through 16)	(9)	472.75
9. We adjust from a prior reporting period (explain in Part 5 - Remarks, on back)			18. We adjust from a prior reporting period (explain in Part 5 - Remarks, on back)	(10)	2.00

Part 2 - Report Period Tax Payments *(See Instructions - Part 2)*

	Return Serial Number	Date Filed	Tax Liability	Adjustments	Amount Paid
(11)	2005-1	1/28/2005	$ 105.00	$ -	$ 105.00
	2005-2	2/5/2005	$ 890.75	$ 14.00	$ 904.75
	2005-3	2/27/2005	$ 546.00	$ -	$ 546.00
	2005-4	3/6/2005	$ 348.25	$ -	$ 348.25
	2005-5	3/29/2005	$ 698.25	$ -	$ 698.25
	2005-6	4/4/2005	$ 675.50	$ -	$ 675.50
			$	$	$

Part 3 - Summary of Materials Used and Wort Produced

Item	Hops (pounds) (a)	Hops Extract (pounds) (b)	Hops Extract Hops Equivalent (c)	Wort (barrels) (d)	Barley specify (e)	Wheat specify (f)	specify (g)	specify (h)
1. Material for beer & cereal beverage	(12) 576				25295	3720		
2. Wort received and used								
3. Wort removed								
4.								

Under penalties of perjury I declare that this report is supported by true, complete, and correct records that are available for inspection at my brewery. I have examined this report and to the best of my knowledge and belief it is true, complete, and correct.

John Smith

Signature	Owner	4/4/05
Signature	Title	Date

Explanation of Entries on Sample "Brewpub Report of Operations"

1. The brewpub produced 470.25 barrels of beer for the quarter.

2. The brewpub received 2 barrels of beer from another brewer of the same owner.

3. One half barrel was returned to the brewery. This beer was destroyed and reported in Line 13. See item 7 below.

4. Line 8 is the total of Lines 1 through 7.

5. The brewpub tax determined 466.25 barrels for use in the tavern.

6. The brewpub transferred 3.75 barrels to another brewery of the same owner.

7. The brewpub destroyed 0.5 barrels at the brewery. This beer was returned to the brewery and reported on Line 4. See item 3 above.

8. The brewpub lost 2.25 barrels of beer, which must be explained in the remarks section.

9. Line 17 is the total of Lines 10 through 16.

10. Line 18 indicates an adjustment of 2 barrels from a previous reporting period. This must be explained in Part 5 – Remarks.

11. The brewpub has filled in all required information for the tax returns covered by this reporting period.

12. The brewpub used 576 pounds of hops, 25,295 pounds of barley and 3720 pounds of wheat in production of their beer.

TTB P 5130.005 (09/2007)

Pay.Gov

TTB P 5130.005 (09/2007)

What is Pay.gov?

ite

ax Returns

xes

rational Reports

es a confirmation number

Why should I use Pay.gov?

PAY.GOV

...ll help reduce the telephone calls to ...plete or correct a form

...elp save time, money, and energy

...o with amending forms

...with penalties and interest

...the system secure?

...s the same systems banks use to ...er their money

...ated Clearing House (ACH)

Did I tell you it is FREE?

You can use the system for

FREE

There is no fee.

TTB P 5130.005 (09/2007)

TTB & Pay.gov Screen

The "Main" Pay.gov screen:

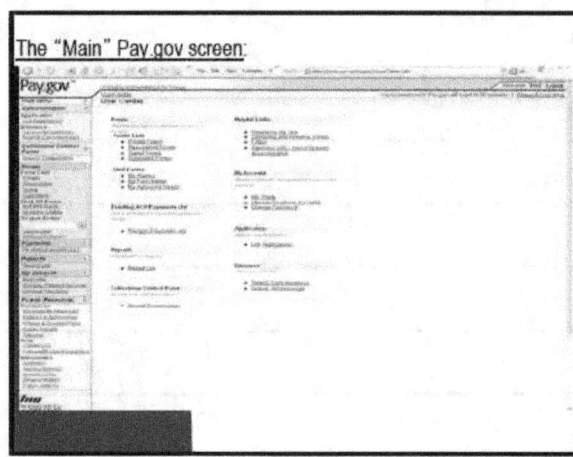

The list of forms available on Pay.gov :

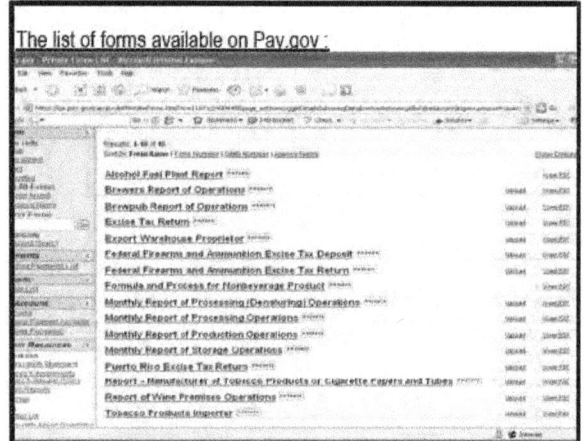

Saved and Submitted Forms

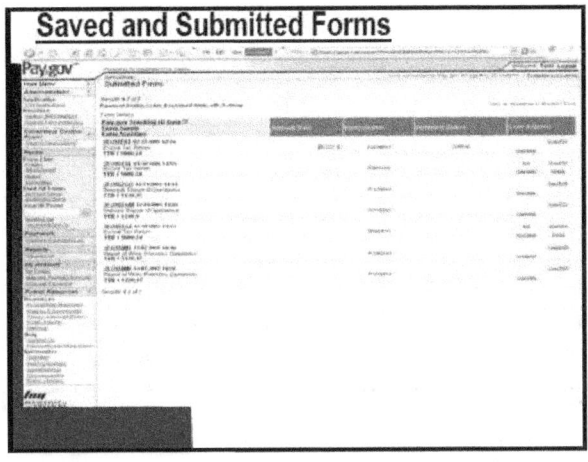

Brewer's Report of Operations

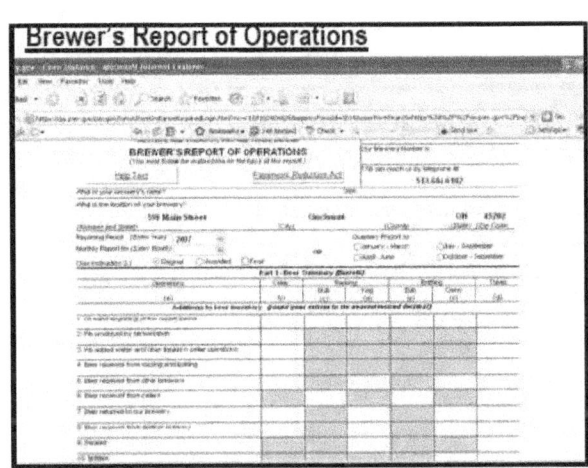

Brewpub Report of Operations

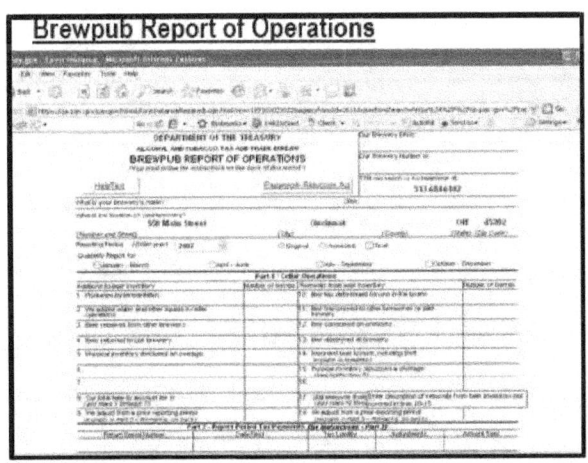

TTB P 5130.005 (09/2007)

The Alcohol and Tobacco Excise Tax Return form on Pay.gov :

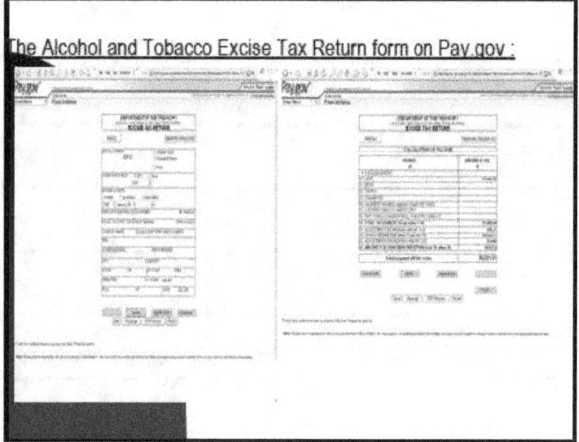

How do I enroll?

Complete an Alcohol & Tobacco Tax and Trade Bureau
(TTB) User Agreement

Agreements can be found at:

(www.ttb.gov/epayment/user_agreement.pdf)

Complete the form with the requested
information, including signature and date,
to obtain a User ID and password

up for multiple Permit/Registry numbers
eement.

Where do I send my form?

user agreement to:

and Tobacco Tax and Trade Bureau (TTB)
.Gov
Street, Room 8002
OH 45202

What happens next?

individual enrolling must have signing
ity for the company.

en sends you a User Identification
wo weeks via e-mail.

receive your User ID and password
riod, contact us at 1-877-882-3277
tb.gov.

Where do I go for help?

- For assistance in completing the User Agreement or
questions about Pay.gov, you can access the system
the TTB web site at
//www.ttb.gov/epayment.htm.

sh Users: Are not supported at this time.
also obtain information and help at these

Alcohol and Tobacco Tax and Trade Bureau
Attn: Pay.gov
550 Main Street - Room 8002
Cincinnati, OH 45202
ne: 1-877-TTB-FAQS (882-3277)
Pay.gov@ttb.gov

TTB P 5130.005 (09/2007)